6/12

W9-BWH-565

DISCARD

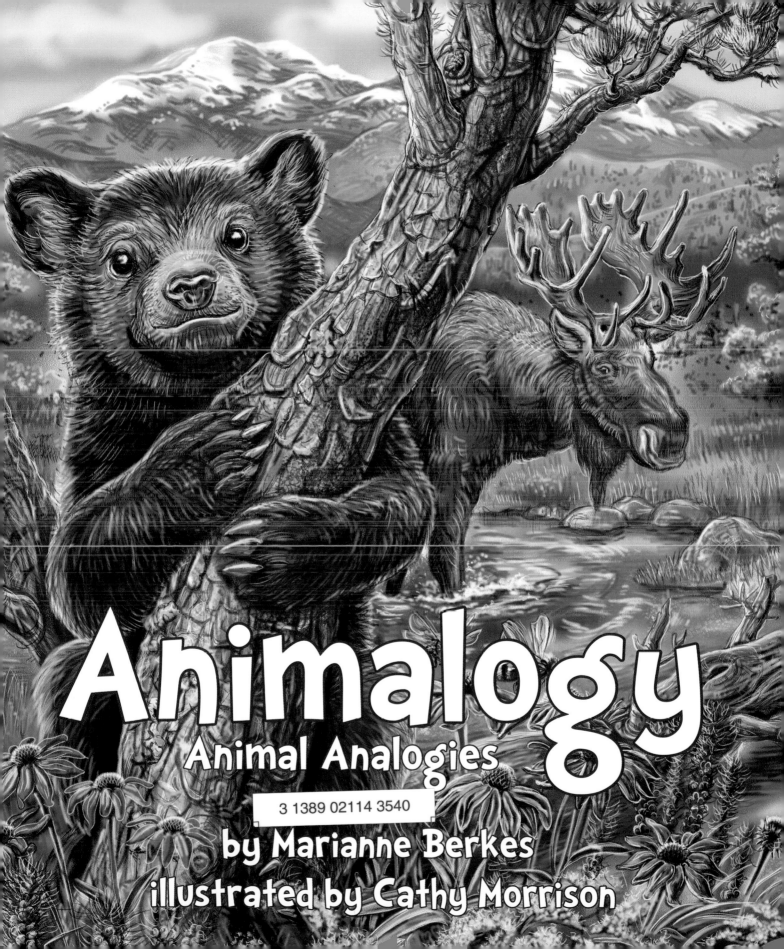

Animalogy
Animal Analogies

by Marianne Berkes

illustrated by Cathy Morrison

Deer is to run,

as mouse is to scurry.

Chick is to feathery,

as bear is to furry.

Rabbit is to nibble,

as skunk is to dig.

Ant is to tiny,

as hippo is to big.

Bat is to flit,

as eagle is to soar.

Dog is to bark,

as lion is to roar.

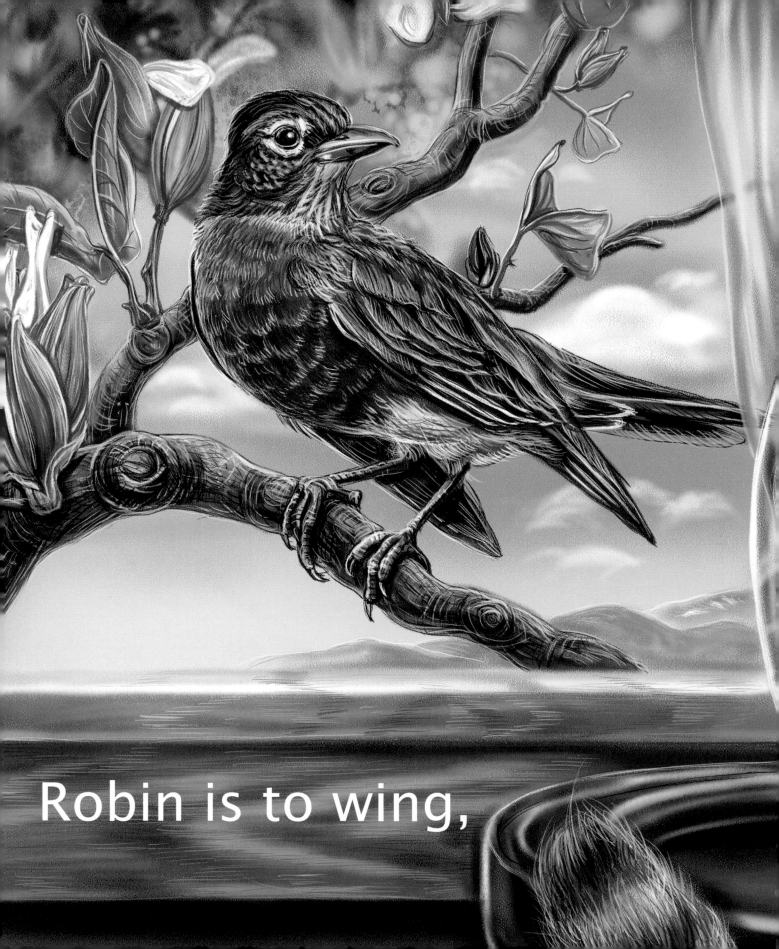

Robin is to wing,

as goldfish is to fin.

Beaver is to build,

as spider is to spin.

Amphibian is to frog,

as mammal is to moose.

Fish is to flounder,

as bird is to goose.

Reptile is to snake,

as insect is to bee.

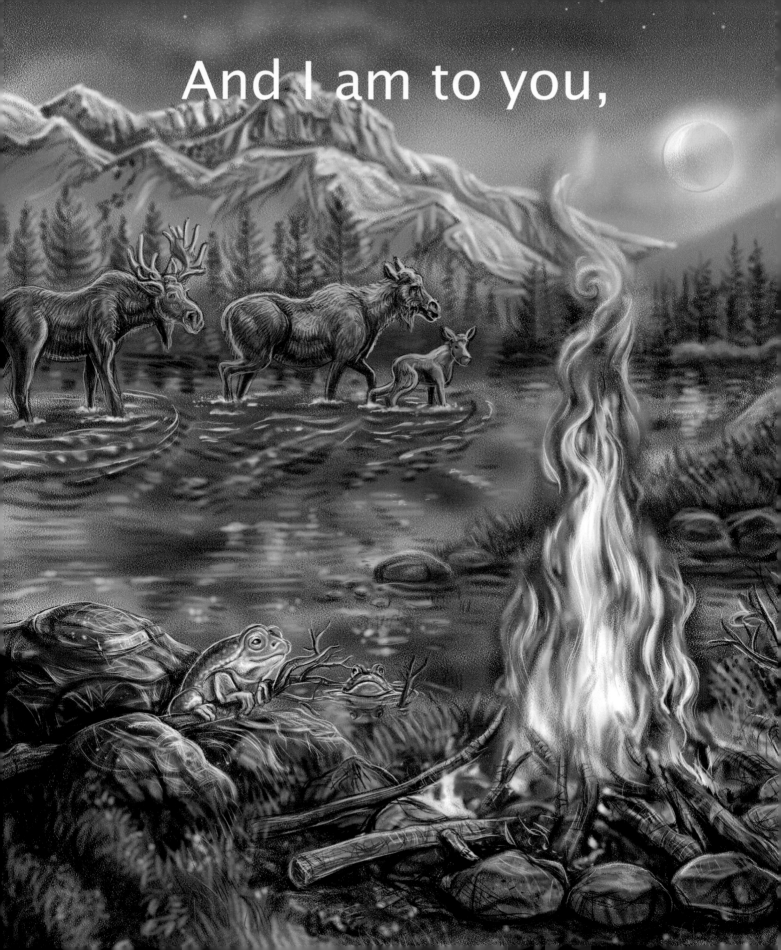

as you are to me!

For Creative Minds

Analogies

Analogies compare or contrast different things to show how they are related to each other. Which of these analogies uses body parts to compare or contrast the animals?

robin: wing :: goldfish: fin

bat: flit :: eagle: soar

Can you come up with other analogies using animal body parts?
How do the animals use those body parts?

 chick's beak

 lion's teeth

 frog's foot

 dog's paws

 skunk's tail

 mouse's tail

 rabbit's ear

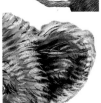 bear's ear

Which of these analogies uses size to compare or contrast the two animals?

deer : run :: mouse : scurry   ant : tiny :: hippo : big

What are some ways we measure things?
What are some other words that describe animal sizes?
Can you come up with other analogies to compare and contrast animal sizes?

tall

long

small

wide

little

short

huge

light   heavy

tiny   giant

Adjectives describe things—like how big or little an animal is.
Which adjectives are alike and which are opposites?

0 Inch   1   2   3   4   5   6   7

Which of these analogies uses action words (verbs) to compare what the animals are doing?

dog : bark :: lion : roar   reptile: snake :: insect: bee

What sounds do other animals make?
Can you come up with other analogies using animal sounds?

Which word (or words) do you think best describes the animal's action?

 Snakes slither, crawl, glide, slide, or wriggle.

 Deer run, jump, bound, dash, spring, sprint, or scamper.

 Eagles soar, glide, or fly.

 Goldfish swim, float, or lap.

 Mice scurry, scamper, or dash.

 Bats flit, fly, glide, flutter, or soar.

 Frogs hop, jump, leap, or vault.

 Beavers cut, build, swim, or munch.

 Robins fly, nest, sing, or tweet.

 Lions, roar, hunt, prey, or chase.

Which of these analogies uses skin coverings to compare or contrast the two animals?

beaver: build :: spider: spin

chick: feathery :: bear: furry

 **1** Which animals have feathers?

 **2** Which animals have hair or fur?

 **3** Which animal has dry scales?

 **4** Which animals have wet (slimy) scales?

 **5** Which animal has smooth, moist skin?

Animal Classification

Vertebrates are animals that have backbones.

Reptiles:
dry scales or plates
lungs to breathe
most hatch from eggs
cold-blooded

Birds:
feathers
lungs to breathe
hatch from eggs
warm-blooded

Mammals:
hair or fur
lungs to breathe
most have live birth
warm-blooded

Amphibians:
soft, moist skin
most young have an aquatic larva/tadpole stage with
gills; adults live on land using lungs to breathe
cold-blooded

Fishes:
most have slime-covered scales
gills to breathe
can have live birth or hatch from eggs
cold-blooded

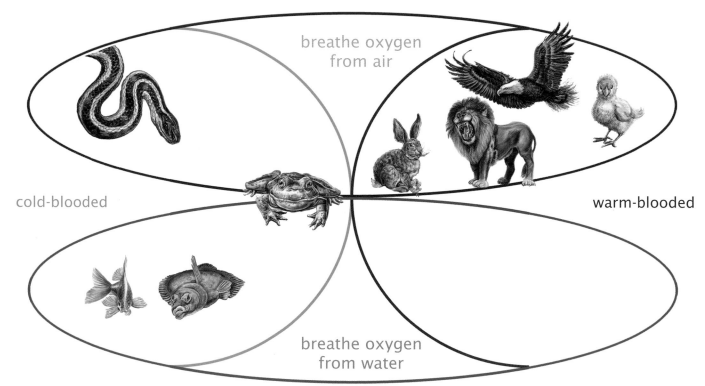

breathe oxygen
from air

cold-blooded

warm-blooded

breathe oxygen
from water

Cold-blooded animals' body temperatures come
from their surroundings.

Warm-blooded animals make their own heat and
have constant body temperatures.

Invertebrates do not have backbones.

Insects:
hard outer covering (exoskeleton)
adults have 3 body parts:
head, thorax & abdomen
3 pairs of legs
usually 2 pairs of wings and 1 pair of antennae
can have live birth or hatch from eggs
cold-blooded

Arachnids (Spiders):
hard outer covering (exoskeleton)
body usually divided into two parts:
cephalothorax and abdomen
4 pairs of legs
no antennae or wings
can have live birth or hatch from eggs
cold-blooded

Animal	Class
frog	amphibian
spider	arachnid
ant	insect
bee	insect
chick	bird
eagle	bird
goose	bird
robin	bird
flounder	fish
goldfish	fish
snake	reptile

Animal	Class
bat	mammal
bear	mammal
beaver	mammal
deer	mammal
dog	mammal
hippo	mammal
lion	mammal
moose	mammal
mouse	mammal
rabbit	mammal
skunk	mammal

1. How many animals in this book are mammals?

2. How many animals in the book are reptiles?

3. How many are fish?

4. Are there any amphibians?

5. Which animals are birds and how many are there?

6. Which animals fly?

7. Are birds the only animals that can fly?

8. What do reptiles, birds, mammals, amphibians and fish all have in common?

9. What do the spider, ant, and bee have in common?

10. Which animals have four legs?

Answers: 1. 11; 2. 1; 3. 2; 4. yes, the frog; 5. chick, eagle, goose, and robin (4 different types); 6. All of the birds fly, plus the bat and bees; 7. No, bats and several insects fly too; 8. They are all vertebrates (have backbones); 9. They are invertebrates, they do not have backbones; 10. frog, bear, beaver, deer, dog, hippo, lion, moose, mouse, rabbit, and skunk

For my granddaughter, Emily Anne, "And I am to your mother, as she is to you." love, Your Oma—MB

To my husband, Andy Brown, who taught our children to love nature—CM

Thanks to Loran Wlodarski, Science Writer at SeaWorld Orlando, for verifying the accuracy of the information in this book.

Library of Congress Cataloging-in-Publication Data

Berkes, Marianne Collins.
Animalogy : animal analogies / by Marianne Berkes ; illustrated by Cathy Morrison.
p. cm.
ISBN 978-1-60718-127-9 (hardcover) -- ISBN 978-1-60718-137-8 (pbk.) -- ISBN 978-1-60718-147-7 (English ebook) -- ISBN 978-1-60718-157-6 (Spanish ebook) 1. Animals--Juvenile literature. 2. Analogy--Juvenile literature. I. Morrison, Cathy. II. Title.
QL49.B5517 2011
590.1--dc22

2011006510

Also available as eBooks featuring auto-flip, auto-read, 3D-page-curling, and selectable English and Spanish text and audio
Interest level: 003-008
Grade level: P-3
Lexile Level: 70 Lexile Code: AD
Curriculum keywords: adaptations, analogies, antonyms/synonyms, compare/contrast, counting, measurements, repeated lines, rhythm or rhyme, classification, word nuances

Manufactured in China, June, 2011
This product conforms to CPSIA 2008
First Printing
Published by Sylvan Dell Publishing
Mt. Pleasant, SC 29464